CROCK·POT®
· THE ORIGINAL SLOW COOKER ·

5 Ingredients or Less!
Dump Meals

Publications International, Ltd.

TELEBrands PRESS

Telebrands Press
79 Two Bridges Road
Fairfield, NJ 07004
www.telebrands.com

Pictured on the front cover: Easy Beef Stew *(page 46)*.
Pictured on the back cover *(top to bottom):* Chicken in Enchilada Sauce *(page 56)*, Fantastic Pot Roast *(page 72)* and Cherry Delight *(page 28)*.

Library of Congress Control Number: 2015936259

ISBN: 978-0-9909635-2-3

Manufactured in China.

8 7 6 5 4 3 2 1

About Cathy: Cathy Mitchell has been cooking for 60 years, starting at her grandmother's side, standing on a stool. She never refers to herself as a chef, but rather a great home cook who enjoys making simple, easy meals with ordinary ingredients. She has been sharing those ideas on television since her first commercial in 1989, introducing America to the electric sandwich maker, and in typical Cathy fashion, making a lot more than sandwiches.

Cathy has an extended family of five adult kids, ranging in age from 31 to 43, and ten grandkids from 1 to 20. One of her favorite stories is overhearing her oldest son's response when a dinner guest commented before dinner that he didn't really like something on the menu. He said, "Well, maybe not before, but you haven't tried my Mom's yet!"

Publications International, Ltd.

TABLE OF CONTENTS

Slow Cooking Hints and Tips _____ 4

Cathy's Favorites _____ 8

Soups, Stews and Chilis _____ 36

Chicken Favorites _____ 54

Bountiful Beef _____ 72

Pleasing Pork _____ 90

Spectacular Sides _____ 108

Sweet Treats _____ 124

Index _____ 140

SLOW COOKING HINTS AND TIPS

Sizes of CROCK-POT® Slow Cookers

Smaller **CROCK-POT®** slow cookers—such as 1- to 3½-quart models—are the perfect size for cooking for singles, a couple or empty nesters (and also for serving dips).

While medium-size **CROCK-POT®** slow cookers (those holding somewhere between 3 quarts and 5 quarts) will easily cook enough food at a time to feed a small family. They are also convenient for holiday side dishes or appetizers.

Large **CROCK-POT®** slow cookers are great for large family dinners, holiday entertaining and potluck suppers. A 6- to 7-quart model is ideal if you like to make meals in advance, or have dinner tonight and store leftovers for another day.

Types of CROCK-POT® Slow Cookers

Current **CROCK-POT®** slow cookers come equipped with many different features and benefits, from auto cook programs to oven-safe stoneware to timed programming. Please

visit **WWW.CROCK-POT.COM** to find the **CROCK-POT®** slow cooker that best suits your needs.

How you plan to use the **CROCK-POT®** slow cooker may affect the model you  choose to purchase. For everyday cooking, choose a size large enough to serve your family. If you plan to use the **CROCK-POT®** slow cooker primarily for entertaining, choose one of the larger sizes. Basic **CROCK-POT®** slow cookers can hold as little as 16 ounces or as much as 7 quarts. The smallest sizes are great for keeping dips warm on a buffet, while the larger sizes can more readily fit large quantities of food and larger roasts.

Cooking, Stirring and Food Safety

CROCK-POT® slow cookers are safe to leave unattended. The outer heating base may get hot, but it should not pose a fire hazard. The heating element in the heating base functions at a low wattage and is safe on countertops.

Your **CROCK-POT®** slow cooker should be filled about one-half to three-fourths full for most recipes unless otherwise instructed. Lean meats such as chicken or pork tenderloin will cook faster than meats with more connective tissue and fat such as beef chuck or pork shoulder. Bone-in meats will take longer than boneless cuts. Typical **CROCK-POT®** slow cooker dishes take approximately 7 to 8 hours to reach the simmer point on LOW and about 3 to 4 hours on HIGH. Once the vegetables and meat start to simmer and braise, their flavors will fully blend and meat will become fall-off-the-bone tender.

According to the U.S. Department of Agriculture, all bacteria are killed at a temperature of 165°F. It's important to follow the recommended cooking times and not to open the lid often, especially early in the cooking process when heat is building up inside the unit. If you need to open the lid to check on your food or are adding additional ingredients, remember to allow additional cooking time if necessary to ensure food is cooked through and tender.

Large **CROCK-POT®** slow cookers, the 6- to 7-quart sizes, may benefit from a quick stir halfway through the cooking time to help distribute heat and promote even cooking. It's usually unnecessary to stir at all, as even ½ cup liquid will help to distribute heat and the stoneware is the perfect medium for holding food at an even temperature throughout the cooking process.

Oven-Safe Stoneware

All **CROCK-POT®** slow cooker removable stoneware inserts may (without their lids) be used safely in ovens at up to 400°F. In addition, all **CROCK-POT®** slow cookers are microwavable without their lids. If you own another slow cooker brand, please refer to your owner's manual for specific stoneware cooking medium tolerances.

Frozen Food

Frozen food can be successfully cooked in a **CROCK-POT®** slow cooker. However, it will require longer cooking time than the same recipe made with fresh food. It's almost always preferable to thaw frozen food prior to placing it in the **CROCK-POT®** slow cooker. Using an instant-read thermometer is recommended to ensure meat is fully cooked.

Pasta and Rice

If you are converting a recipe for a **CROCK-POT®** slow cooker that calls for uncooked pasta, first cook the pasta on the stove top just until slightly tender. Then add the pasta to the **CROCK-POT®** slow cooker. If you are converting a recipe for the **CROCK-POT®** slow cooker that calls for cooked rice, stir in raw rice with the other recipe ingredients plus ¼ cup extra liquid per ¼ cup of raw rice.

Beans

Beans must be softened completely before combining with sugar and/or acidic foods in the **CROCK-POT®** slow cooker. Sugar and acid have a hardening effect on beans and will prevent softening. Fully cooked canned beans may be used as a substitute for dried beans.

Vegetables

Root vegetables often cook more slowly than meat. Cut vegetables accordingly to cook at the same rate as meat—large or small or lean versus marbled—and place near the sides or bottom of the stoneware to facilitate cooking.

Herbs

Fresh herbs add flavor and color when added at the end of the cooking cycle; if added at the beginning, many fresh herbs' flavor will dissipate over long cook times. Ground and/or dried herbs and spices work well in slow cooking and may be added at the beginning of cook time. For dishes with shorter cook times, hearty fresh herbs such as rosemary and thyme hold up well. The flavor power of all herbs and spices can vary greatly depending on their particular strength and shelf life. Use chili powders and garlic powder sparingly, as these can sometimes intensify over the long cook times. Always taste the finished dish and correct seasonings including salt and pepper.

Liquids

It's not necessary to use more than ½ to 1 cup liquid in most instances since juices in meats and vegetables are retained more in slow cooking than in conventional cooking. Excess liquid can be cooked down and concentrated after slow cooking on the stove top or by removing meat and vegetables from stoneware, stirring in a thickeners (flour, cornstarch or tapioca) and setting the **CROCK-POT®** slow cooker to HIGH. Cover; cook on HIGH for approximately 15 minutes or until juices are thickened.

Milk

Milk, cream and sour cream break down during extended cooking.

When possible, add them during the last 15 to 30 minutes of slow cooking, until just heated through. Condensed soups may be substituted for milk and may cook for extended times.

Fish

Fish is delicate and should be added or gently stirred into the **CROCK-POT®** slow cooker during the last 15 to 30 minutes of cooking time. Cover; cook just until cooked through.

Baked Goods

To prepare bread or cakes in a **CROCK-POT®** slow cooker, you may want to purchase a covered, vented metal cake pan accessory. You can also use any straight-sided soufflé dish or deep cake pan that will fit into the stoneware. Baked goods can also be prepared directly in the stoneware; however, they can be a little difficult to remove from the insert, so follow the recipe carefully.

CROCK-POT® Slow Cooker Recipes with 5 Ingredients or Less

A well-stocked pantry is a shortcut to preparing dishes and entire meals efficiently. This cookbook takes full advantage of the kinds of everyday ingredients most cooks commonly have on hand. It features recipes that can be created with 5 ingredients and/or the addition of these common pantry items:

- Water

- Milk

- Eggs

- Butter

- Vegetable oil

- Olive oil

- Onions and garlic

- Other common spices (such as ground cinnamon, ground nutmeg, ground red pepper, red pepper flakes, garlic powder, ground cumin, ground oregano, dried thyme, chili powder, paprika, etc.)

- Salt and black pepper

- All-purpose flour

- Arrowroot

- Granulated sugar

- Brown sugar

These slow-cooked recipes are perfect for busy days when you don't have time to make another stop at the grocery store.

CATHY'S FAVORITES

Tender Pot Roast

Makes 8 servings

Assorted vegetables (potatoes, carrots, onions and celery)

1 boneless beef chuck shoulder roast (3 to 4 pounds), trimmed*

3 cups water

1 package (about 1 ounce) dry onion soup mix

1 package (about 1 ounce) au jus gravy mix

1 package (about 1 ounce) mushroom gravy mix

*Unless you have a 5-, 6- or 7-quart **CROCK-POT®** slow cooker, cut any roast larger than 2½ pounds in half so it cooks completely.*

Combine vegetables, beef, water, dry soup mix and gravy mixes in **CROCK-POT®** slow cooker; turn beef to coat. Cover; cook on LOW 8 hours or on HIGH 4 hours.

Tomato Sauce with Meatballs and Sausage

Makes 6 to 8 servings

2 packages (about 16 ounces *each*) frozen fully cooked meatballs, partially thawed and separated

1 package (19 ounces) Italian sausage, cooked and cut into 1-inch slices

1 can (28 ounces) peeled whole tomatoes

½ cup chopped fresh basil

2 tablespoons olive oil

2 cloves garlic, finely minced

1 teaspoon sugar

Salt and black pepper

Hot cooked spaghetti (optional)

Combine meatballs, sausage, tomatoes, basil, oil, garlic, sugar, salt and pepper in **CROCK-POT®** slow cooker; stir to blend. Cover; cook on LOW 3 to 5 hours or on HIGH 2 to 4 hours. Serve over pasta, if desired.

Root Beer BBQ Pulled Pork

Makes 8 servings

1 (6- to 8-pound) boneless pork shoulder roast*

1 bottle (18 ounces) sweet barbecue sauce

1 can (12 ounces) root beer

1 package (1 ounce) dry onion soup mix

Salt and black pepper

Hamburger buns (optional)

Potato chips and pickles (optional)

*Unless you have a 5-, 6- or 7-quart **CROCK-POT**® slow cooker, cut any roast larger than 2½ pounds in half so it cooks completely.*

1. Coat inside of **CROCK-POT**® slow cooker with nonstick cooking spray.

2. Combine pork, barbecue sauce, root beer, dry soup mix, salt and pepper in **CROCK-POT**® slow cooker; turn pork to coat. Cover; cook on LOW 8 to 10 hours.

3. Remove pork to large cutting board; shred with two forks. Serve on buns, if desired. Serve with chips and pickles, if desired.

Root Beer BBQ Pulled Pork

Best Barbecued Ribs

Makes 6 to 8 servings

2½ pounds pork baby back ribs, silver skin removed

1 can (20 ounces) beer or beef broth

1 bottle (18 ounces) barbecue sauce

½ cup honey

Sesame seeds and fresh chopped chives (optional)

Stand meaty side of ribs around side of **CROCK-POT**® slow cooker. Pour in beer, barbecue sauce and honey. Cover; cook on LOW 6 to 7 hours or on HIGH 3 to 3½ hours. Garnish with sesame seeds and chives.

CATHY'S TIP:

The ribs will take on additional browning from the **CROCK-POT**® slow cooker if you stand them up around the side as the recipe directs.

Best Barbecued Ribs

Cinnamon Roll-Topped Mixed Berry Cobbler

Makes 8 servings

2 bags (12 ounces *each*) frozen mixed berries, thawed

1 cup sugar

¼ cup quick-cooking tapioca

¼ cup water

2 teaspoons vanilla

1 package (about 12 ounces) refrigerated cinnamon rolls
   with icing

Combine berries, sugar, tapioca, water and vanilla in **CROCK-POT®**
slow cooker; top with cinnamon rolls. Cover; cook on LOW 4 to
5 hours. Serve warm, drizzled with icing.

Note: This recipe was designed to work best in a 5-quart **CROCK-POT®**
slow cooker. Double the ingredients for larger **CROCK-POT®** slow
cookers, but always place cinnamon rolls in a single layer.

Cinnamon Roll-Topped Mixed Berry Cobbler

Chicken Soft Tacos

Makes 4 servings

3 bell peppers (green, red and yellow), sliced

1 large onion, sliced

1 pound boneless, skinless chicken breasts

1 (1-ounce) package taco seasoning mix

Corn or flour tortillas

Optional toppings: salsa, sour cream, cheese, guacamole, lettuce and/or tomatoes

1. Layer bell peppers, onions, chicken and taco seasoning mix in **CROCK-POT®** slow cooker. Cover; cook on LOW 6 to 8 hours or on HIGH 3 to 4 hours.

2. Remove chicken to large cutting board; shred with two forks. Serve on tortillas with desired toppings.

Chicken Soft Tacos

Smothered Pork Chops and Rice

Makes 4 servings

1 cup uncooked rice

4 (¾-inch-thick) pork chops

1 can (10¾ ounces) cream of mushroom soup

2 soup cans of water

1 (1-ounce) package dry onion soup mix

Corn on the cob (optional)

Layer rice, pork, soup, water and dry soup mix in **CROCK-POT®** slow cooker. Cover; cook on LOW 8 hours or on HIGH 4 hours. Serve with corn, if desired.

Smothered Pork Chops and Rice

Ginger Teriyaki Chicken

Makes 4 to 6 servings

3½ to 4 pounds chicken thighs and drumsticks

1 can (15 ounces) baby corn (optional)

1 can (12 ounces) ginger ale

1 bottle (10 ounces) teriyaki sauce

1 cup uncooked long grain rice

2 cups very hot water

1 teaspoon salt

2 teaspoons sesame seeds and shredded carrots (optional)

1. Place small metal bowl in bottom of **CROCK-POT®** slow cooker. Place chicken around bowl; top with corn, if desired. Pour ginger ale and teriyaki sauce over chicken. Combine rice, water and salt in bowl. Cover; cook on HIGH 4 hours or until chicken is cooked through.

2. Serve chicken over rice. Garnish with sesame seeds and carrots.

Family Tortilla Bowl

Makes 8 servings

Nonstick cooking spray

8 (6-inch) flour tortillas

1½ cups (6 ounces) shredded Cheddar cheese

1 pound ground beef, cooked and drained

1 can (about 15 ounces) black or pinto beans, drained

⅓ cup taco sauce

Optional toppings: black olives, sliced jalapeño peppers, shredded lettuce, tomato slices, avocado slices, sour cream, guacamole and/or salsa

1. Spray both sides of each tortilla with cooking spray. Prepare foil handles.*

2. Place 4 tortillas in bottom and extending up sides of **CROCK-POT®** slow cooker, forming a bowl. Layer one third of cheese, half of beef, half of beans and half of taco sauce over tortillas. Layer 2 tortillas, one third of cheese, remaining half of beef and beans. Top with remaining half of taco sauce, remaining 2 tortillas and remaining one third of cheese.

3. Cover; cook on HIGH 3 hours or until tortillas are crispy and cheese is melted. Remove from **CROCK-POT®** slow cooker using foil handles. Cut into eight wedges. Serve with desired toppings.

*To make foil handles, tear off three 18×2-inch strips of heavy-duty foil or use regular foil folded to double thickness. Crisscross foil strips in spoke design and place in **CROCK-POT®** slow cooker.

Cheesy Dump Pizza

Makes 8 servings

1 package (7½ ounces) refrigerated biscuits (10 biscuits), each biscuit cut into 6 pieces

1 cup (4 ounces) shredded mozzarella cheese

1 cup marinara or pizza sauce

Optional toppings: pepperoni, sausage, black olives, mushrooms and/or chopped bell peppers

1. Prepare foil handles.*

2. Layer biscuit pieces, half of cheese, marinara sauce, toppings, if desired, and remaining half of cheese in **CROCK-POT®** slow cooker. Cover; cook on HIGH 3 hours.

3. Remove from **CROCK-POT®** slow cooker, using foil handles. Cut into eight wedges.

To make foil handles, tear off three 18×2-inch strips of heavy-duty foil or use regular foil folded to double thickness. Crisscross foil strips in spoke design and place in **CROCK-POT® slow cooker.*

Ranch Chicken and Stuffing

Makes 4 to 6 servings

4 to 6 boneless, skinless chicken breasts

1 package (1 ounce) ranch seasoning mix

1 package (12 ounces) chicken flavor stuffing mix

1 package (about 8 ounces) frozen mixed vegetables (carrots and peas)

1½ cups chicken broth

Sprigs fresh thyme (optional)

Steamed carrots (optional)

1. Coat inside of **CROCK-POT®** slow cooker with nonstick cooking spray.

2. Place chicken in bottom of **CROCK-POT®** slow cooker; sprinkle with seasoning mix. Pour in stuffing mix, mixed vegetables and broth. Cover; cook on LOW 8 hours or on HIGH 4 hours. Garnish with thyme. Serve with carrots, if desired.

Cherry Delight

Makes 8 to 10 servings

1 can (21 ounces) cherry pie filling

1 package (about 18 ounces) yellow cake mix

½ cup (1 stick) butter, melted

⅓ cup chopped walnuts

1. Coat inside of **CROCK-POT®** slow cooker with nonstick cooking spray.

2. Pour pie filling into **CROCK-POT®** slow cooker. Combine cake mix and butter in medium bowl. Spread evenly over pie filling. Sprinkle with walnuts. Cover; cook on LOW 3 to 4 hours or on HIGH 1½ to 2 hours.

One Pot Meatloaf Dinner

Makes 6 servings

1 pound ground beef

½ pound ground pork

2 eggs

1 small onion, chopped (about ½ cup)

½ medium green bell pepper, chopped (about ½ cup)

¾ cup oats

1 can (4 ounces) tomato sauce, divided

Salt and black pepper

6 baking potatoes

1. Combine beef, pork, eggs, onion, bell pepper, oats, half of tomato sauce, salt and black pepper in large bowl; mix well. Press mixture into 9×5-inch baking pan; top with remaining half of tomato sauce.

2. Wrap potatoes in foil; place in bottom of **CROCK-POT**® slow cooker. Place meatloaf on top of potatoes. Cover; cook on LOW 7 to 8 hours or on HIGH 3 to 4 hours or until meatloaf is firm and cooked through.

3. Remove meatloaf to large cutting board; let stand 5 minutes before slicing. Serve meatloaf with potatoes.

CATHY'S TIP:

To make cleanup easier, combine the beef, pork, eggs, onion, bell pepper, oats, half of tomato sauce, salt and black pepper in large resealable food storage bag; mix well. Then you can simply press the mixture into the 9×5-inch pan, using the bag. Continue as recipe directs.

Triple Chocolate Brownies

Makes 6 servings

2½ cups packaged brownie mix

½ cup milk chocolate chips

½ cup packed brown sugar

½ cup very hot water

2 eggs, beaten

3 tablespoons butter, melted

1 package (2¾ ounces) instant chocolate pudding mix

2 tablespoons unsweetened cocoa powder

Whipped cream or ice cream (optional)

1. Coat inside of **CROCK-POT®** slow cooker with nonstick cooking spray.

2. Combine brownie mix, chocolate chips, brown sugar, water, eggs, butter, pudding mix and cocoa in **CROCK-POT®** slow cooker; stir to blend. Cover; cook on HIGH 2 hours.

3. Turn off heat. Let stand 30 minutes. Top with whipped cream, if desired.

Juicy Roasted Chicken

Makes 8 to 10 servings

1 large onion, sliced

5 red potatoes, cut into halves

1 bag (16 ounces) baby carrots

1 bag (12 ounces) frozen broccoli

1 (6- to 7-pound) whole chicken

1 tablespoon seasoned salt

1 tablespoon paprika

1 tablespoon black pepper

Sprigs fresh rosemary (optional)

1. Place onion in bottom of **CROCK-POT®** slow cooker. Prepare foil handles.*

2. Add potatoes, carrots and broccoli over foil handles. Season chicken with salt, paprika and pepper; add to **CROCK-POT®** slow cooker. Cover; cook on LOW 8 hours or until chicken is cooked through.

3. Remove chicken from **CROCK-POT®** slow cooker using foil handles. Cover loosely with clean foil; let stand 10 to 15 minutes before cutting into pieces. Garnish with rosemary.

To make foil handles, tear off three 18×2-inch strips of heavy-duty foil or use regular foil folded to double thickness. Crisscross foil strips in spoke design and place in **CROCK-POT® slow cooker.*

Juicy Roasted Chicken

CATHY'S TIP:

To determine if the chicken is thoroughly cooked and ready to eat, insert a meat thermometer into the thickest part of the thigh, but not near any bone or fat. It should register 180°F before removing the chicken from the **CROCK-POT®** slow cooker.

SOUPS, STEWS AND CHILIS

Simmered Split Pea Soup

Makes 6 servings

3 cans (about 14 ounces *each*) chicken broth

1 package (16 ounces) dried split peas, rinsed and sorted

8 slices bacon, crisp-cooked, chopped and divided

1 onion, chopped

2 carrots, chopped

1 teaspoon black pepper

½ teaspoon dried thyme

1 whole bay leaf

Crusty bread (optional)

Combine broth, peas, half of bacon, onion, carrots, pepper, thyme and bay leaf in **CROCK-POT**® slow cooker. Cover; cook on LOW 6 to 8 hours. Remove and discard bay leaf. Garnish with remaining half of bacon. Serve with bread, if desired.

Black and White Chili

Makes 6 servings

1 pound boneless, skinless chicken breasts, cut into ¾-inch
　　pieces

1 can (about 15 ounces) Great Northern beans, rinsed and
　　drained

1 can (about 15 ounces) black beans, rinsed and drained

1 can (about 14 ounces) stewed tomatoes

1 cup chopped onion

2 tablespoons Texas-style chili seasoning mix

Combine chicken, beans, tomatoes, onion and chili seasoning mix in
CROCK-POT® slow cooker; stir to blend. Cover; cook on LOW 4 to
4½ hours.

Black and White Chili

Posole

Makes 8 servings

3 pounds boneless pork, cubed

2 cans (about 15 ounces *each*) white hominy, drained

1 package (10 ounces) frozen white corn, thawed

¾ cup chili sauce

Fresh Italian parsley (optional)

Combine pork, hominy, corn and chili sauce in **CROCK-POT®** slow cooker; stir to blend. Cover; cook on LOW 10 hours or on HIGH 5 hours. Garnish with parsley.

Veggie Soup with Beef

Makes 4 servings

2 cans (15 ounces *each*) mixed vegetables

1 pound cubed beef stew meat

1 can (8 ounces) tomato sauce

2 cloves garlic, minced

Combine vegetables, beef, tomato sauce, garlic and enough water to fill **CROCK-POT®** slow cooker to within ½ inch of top; stir to blend. Cover; cook on LOW 8 to 10 hours.

Mushroom-Beef Stew

Makes 4 servings

1 pound cubed beef stew meat

1 can (10¾ ounces) condensed cream of mushroom soup,
   undiluted

2 cans (4 ounces *each*) sliced mushrooms, drained

1 package (1 ounce) dry onion soup mix

   Hot cooked noodles (optional)

Combine beef, soup, mushrooms and soup mix in **CROCK-POT®**
slow cooker; stir to blend. Cover; cook on LOW 8 to 10 hours. Serve
over noodles, if desired.

Hearty Vegetable and Potato Chowder

Makes 6 servings

2 cups vegetable broth

1 can (10¾ ounces) condensed cream of mushroom soup

1 package (10 ounces) frozen mixed vegetables (corn, carrots, peas and green beans)

½ (32-ounce) package diced hash brown potatoes

2 to 3 teaspoons minced garlic

1½ teaspoons dried thyme

½ teaspoon black pepper

Shredded Colby-Jack or Cheddar cheese (optional)

1. Coat inside of **CROCK-POT®** slow cooker with nonstick cooking spray. Add broth, soup, mixed vegetables, potatoes, garlic, thyme and pepper to **CROCK-POT®** slow cooker; stir to blend. Cover; cook on LOW 7 to 8 hours or on HIGH 3 to 4 hours.

2. Stir to blend. Top each serving with cheese, if desired.

Rustic Vegetable Soup

Makes 8 servings

1 jar (16 ounces) picante sauce

1 package (10 ounces) frozen mixed vegetables

1 package (10 ounces) frozen cut green beans

1 can (about 10 ounces) condensed beef broth, undiluted

½ (28-ounce) package O'Brien potatoes

½ teaspoon sugar

¼ cup finely chopped fresh Italian parsley (optional)

Pretzel rolls (optional)

1. Combine picante sauce, mixed vegetables, green beans, broth, potatoes and sugar in **CROCK-POT®** slow cooker; stir to blend. Cover; cook on LOW 8 hours or on HIGH 4 hours.

2. Garnish with parsley. Serve with rolls, if desired.

Rustic Vegetable Soup

Easy Beef Stew

Makes 6 to 8 servings

1½ to 2 pounds cubed beef stew meat

4 medium potatoes, cubed

4 carrots, cut into 1½-inch pieces *or* 4 cups baby carrots

1 medium onion, cut into 8 pieces

2 cans (8 ounces *each*) tomato sauce

1 teaspoon salt

½ teaspoon black pepper

Combine beef, potatoes, carrots, onion, tomato sauce, salt and pepper in **CROCK-POT®** slow cooker; stir to blend. Cover; cook on LOW 8 to 10 hours.

Navy Bean and Ham Soup

Makes 6 servings

6 cups water

2 cans (about 15 ounces *each*) navy beans, rinsed and drained

1 pound ham, cubed

1 can (about 15 ounces) corn, drained

1 can (about 4 ounces) diced mild green chiles, drained

1 onion, diced

Salt and black pepper

Combine water, beans, ham, corn, chiles, onion, salt and pepper in **CROCK-POT®** slow cooker; stir to blend. Cover; cook on LOW 8 to 10 hours.

Chicken and Wild Rice Soup

Makes 9 servings

3 cans (about 14 ounces *each*) chicken broth

1 pound boneless, skinless chicken breasts or thighs, cut into 1-inch pieces

2 cups water

1 cup sliced celery

1 cup diced carrots

1 package (6 ounces) converted long grain and wild rice mix with seasoning packet (not quick-cooking or instant rice)

½ cup chopped onion

½ teaspoon black pepper

1 tablespoon dried parsley flakes (optional)

Combine broth, chicken, water, celery, carrots, rice and seasoning packet, onion and pepper in **CROCK-POT®** slow cooker; stir to blend. Cover; cook on LOW 6 to 7 hours or on HIGH 4 to 5 hours. Garnish with parsley.

Chicken and Wild Rice Soup

Swiss Steak Stew

Makes 10 servings

- 4 pounds boneless beef top sirloin steaks, each cut into 3 to 4 pieces
- 2 cans (about 14 ounces *each*) diced tomatoes
- 2 medium green bell peppers, cut into ½-inch strips
- 2 medium yellow onions, chopped
- 1 tablespoon seasoned salt
- 1 teaspoon black pepper

Combine beef, tomatoes, bell peppers, onions, salt and black pepper in **CROCK-POT®** slow cooker; stir to blend. Cover; cook on LOW 8 hours.

Clam Chowder

Makes 10 servings

5 cans (10¾ ounces *each*) condensed cream of potato soup, undiluted

2 cans (12 ounces *each*) evaporated milk

2 cans (10 ounces *each*) whole baby clams, rinsed and drained

1 can (14¾ ounces) cream-style corn

2 cans (4 ounces *each*) tiny shrimp, rinsed and drained

¾ cup bacon, crisp-cooked and crumbled (about ½ pound)

Lemon-pepper seasoning

Oyster crackers (optional)

Combine soup, evaporated milk, clams, corn, shrimp, bacon and lemon-pepper seasoning in **CROCK-POT®** slow cooker; stir to blend. Cover; cook on LOW 3 to 4 hours. Serve with oyster crackers, if desired.

Note: Chowder is a milk- or cream-based soup closely associated with New England. It's most often made with clams, but lobster and cod are other favored seafood ingredients.

Corn and Two Bean Chili

Makes 4 servings

1 can (about 15 ounces) pinto or kidney beans, rinsed and drained

1 can (about 15 ounces) black beans, rinsed and drained

1 can (about 14 ounces) fire-roasted diced tomatoes

1 cup salsa

1 cup frozen corn

½ cup minced onion

1 teaspoon chili powder

1 teaspoon ground cumin

Sour cream and shredded Cheddar cheese (optional)

1. Coat inside of **CROCK-POT®** slow cooker with nonstick cooking spray.

2. Combine beans, tomatoes, salsa, corn, onion, chili powder and cumin in **CROCK-POT®** slow cooker; stir to blend. Cover; cook on LOW 5 to 6 hours or on HIGH 2½ to 3 hours. Top each serving with sour cream and cheese, if desired.

Chicken Stew

Makes 6 servings

4 to 5 cups chopped cooked chicken

1 can (28 ounces) whole tomatoes, cut up and undrained

½ (32-ounce) package diced hash brown potatoes

1 can (14¾ ounces) cream-style corn

8 ounces fresh okra, sliced

1 large onion, chopped

½ cup ketchup

½ cup barbecue sauce

Combine chicken, tomatoes, potatoes, corn, okra, onion, ketchup and barbecue sauce in **CROCK-POT®** slow cooker; stir to blend. Cover; cook on LOW 6 to 8 hours.

CHICKEN FAVORITES

Autumn Chicken

Makes 12 servings

1 can (14 ounces) whole artichoke hearts, drained

1 can (14 ounces) whole mushrooms

12 boneless, skinless chicken breasts

1 jar (6½ ounces) marinated artichoke hearts, undrained

¾ cup dry white wine

½ cup balsamic vinaigrette

Hot cooked noodles (optional)

Paprika and chopped fresh basil (optional)

1. Spread whole artichokes over bottom of **CROCK-POT®** slow cooker. Top with half of mushrooms. Layer chicken over mushrooms. Add marinated artichoke hearts with liquid. Add remaining mushrooms. Pour in wine and vinaigrette. Cover; cook on LOW 4 to 5 hours.

2. Serve over noodles, if desired. Garnish with paprika and basil.

Chicken in Enchilada Sauce

Makes 4 servings

1½ pounds boneless, skinless chicken thighs, cut into
    1-inch pieces

1 can (about 14 ounces) diced tomatoes with chipotle
    peppers*

1 can (10 ounces) enchilada sauce

1 cup frozen or canned corn

2 tablespoons minced fresh cilantro

¼ teaspoon ground cumin

¼ teaspoon black pepper

Shredded pepper jack cheese and sliced green onions
    (optional)**

Tortilla chips and lime wedges (optional)

If tomatoes with chipotle peppers are not available, use diced tomatoes with mild green chiles or plain diced tomatoes plus ¼ teaspoon red pepper flakes.

**For a less spicy dish, use Monterey Jack cheese.*

1. Combine chicken, tomatoes, enchilada sauce, corn, cilantro, cumin and pepper in **CROCK-POT®** slow cooker; stir to blend. Cover; cook on LOW 6 to 7 hours.

2. Sprinkle with cheese and green onions, if desired. Serve with chips and lime, if desired.

Spicy Orange Chicken Nuggets

Makes 8 to 9 servings

1 bag (28 ounces) frozen popcorn chicken bites

1½ cups prepared honey teriyaki marinade

¾ cup orange juice concentrate

⅔ cup water

1 tablespoon orange marmalade

½ teaspoon hot chile sauce or sriracha*

Orange peel (optional)

Hot cooked rice with peas and corn (optional)

Sriracha is a Thai hot sauce and is available in Asian specialty markets and large supermarkets.

1. Combine chicken, teriyaki marinade, orange juice concentrate, water, marmalade and chile sauce in **CROCK-POT®** slow cooker; stir to blend. Cover; cook on LOW 3 to 3½ hours.

2. Sprinkle with orange peel and serve with rice, if desired.

Spicy Orange Chicken Nuggets

Chicken and Rice

Makes 4 servings

3 cans (10¾ ounces *each*) condensed cream of chicken soup, undiluted

1 pound boneless, skinless chicken breasts, cut into 1-inch pieces

2 cups uncooked instant rice

1 cup water

½ cup diced celery

½ teaspoon salt

¼ teaspoon black pepper

¼ teaspoon paprika

Combine soup, chicken, rice, water, celery, salt, pepper and paprika in **CROCK-POT®** slow cooker; stir to blend. Cover; cook on LOW 6 to 8 hours or on HIGH 3 to 4 hours.

Chicken and Butternut Squash

Makes 6 servings

6 boneless, skinless chicken thighs (1½ pounds total)

1 (1½- to 2-pound) butternut squash, cubed

2 tablespoons balsamic vinegar

4 cloves garlic, minced

6 fresh sage leaves

Salt and black pepper

Combine chicken, squash, vinegar, garlic, sage, salt and pepper in **CROCK-POT®** slow cooker; stir to blend. Cover; cook on LOW 4 to 6 hours.

Chicken in Honey Sauce

Makes 6 servings

6 boneless, skinless chicken breasts (about 1½ pounds)

2 cups honey

1 cup soy sauce

½ cup ketchup

¼ cup vegetable oil

2 cloves garlic, minced

Salt and black pepper

Sesame seeds (optional)

1. Combine chicken, honey, soy sauce, ketchup, oil, garlic, salt and pepper in **CROCK-POT®** slow cooker. Cover; cook on LOW 6 to 8 hours or on HIGH 3 to 4 hours.

2. Garnish with sesame seeds. Serve with sauce.

Spicy Shredded Chicken

Makes 6 servings

6 boneless, skinless chicken breasts (about 1½ pounds)

1 jar (16 ounces) salsa

Flour tortillas, warmed

Optional toppings: shredded cheese, sour cream, shredded lettuce, diced tomato, diced onion and/or sliced avocado

1. Place chicken in **CROCK-POT®** slow cooker; top with salsa. Cover; cook on LOW 6 to 8 hours.

2. Remove chicken to large cutting board; shred with two forks. Serve in tortillas. Top as desired.

Dijon Chicken Thighs with Artichoke Sauce

Makes 8 servings

2½ pounds skinless chicken thighs (about 8)

1 cup chopped onion

1 can (4 ounces) sliced mushrooms, drained

1 jar (12 ounces) quartered marinated artichoke hearts, undrained

½ cup Dijon mustard

2 tablespoons chopped garlic

½ teaspoon dried tarragon

Hot cooked fettuccine (optional)

Chopped fresh Italian parsley and butter (optional)

Combine chicken, onion, mushrooms, artichokes, mustard, garlic and tarragon in **CROCK-POT®** slow cooker. Cover; cook on LOW 6 to 8 hours or on HIGH 4 hours. Serve over fettuccine tossed with parsley and butter, if desired.

Note: To skin chicken easily, grasp skin with paper towel and pull away. Repeat with fresh paper towel for each piece of chicken, discarding skins and towels.

Mile-High Enchilada Pie

Makes 4 to 6 servings

6 (6-inch) corn tortillas

1 jar (12 ounces) salsa

1 can (about 15 ounces) kidney beans, rinsed and drained

1 cup shredded cooked chicken

1 cup (4 ounces) shredded Monterey Jack cheese with jalapeño peppers

Chopped fresh cilantro and sliced red bell pepper (optional)

1. Prepare foil handles by tearing off three 18×2-inch strips heavy-duty foil (or use regular foil folded to double thickness). Crisscross foil strips in spoke design; place in **CROCK-POT®** slow cooker.

2. Place 1 tortilla on top of foil handles. Top with small amount of salsa, beans, chicken and cheese. Continue layering in order using remaining ingredients, ending with tortilla and cheese. Cover; cook on LOW 6 to 8 hours or on HIGH 3 to 4 hours.

3. Pull pie out by foil handles. Garnish with fresh cilantro and sliced red bell pepper.

Chicken Provençal

Makes 8 servings

2 pounds boneless, skinless chicken thighs, cut into quarters

2 medium red bell peppers, cut into ¼-inch-thick slices

1 medium yellow bell pepper, cut into ¼-inch-thick slices

1 onion, thinly sliced

1 can (28 ounces) plum tomatoes, drained

3 cloves garlic, minced

¼ teaspoon *each* salt, dried thyme and ground fennel seed

3 strips orange peel

½ cup fresh basil leaves, chopped (optional)

Crusty French baguette (optional)

Combine chicken, bell peppers, onion, tomatoes, garlic, salt, thyme, fennel seed and orange peel in **CROCK-POT®** slow cooker; stir to blend. Cover; cook on LOW 7 to 9 hours or on HIGH 4 to 6 hours. Sprinkle with basil, if desired.

Cheesy Slow Cooker Chicken

Makes 6 servings

2 cans (10½ ounces *each*) condensed cream of chicken soup, undiluted

1 can (10½ ounces) condensed Cheddar cheese soup, undiluted

6 boneless, skinless chicken breasts (about 1½ pounds)

Salt and black pepper

Garlic powder

Combine soups in **CROCK-POT®** slow cooker. Add chicken, salt, pepper and garlic powder. Cover; cook on LOW 6 to 8 hours.

Chicken Provençal

Like Grandma's
Chicken 'n' Dumplings

Makes 4 to 6 servings

2 cups cooked chicken

1 can (10½ ounces) condensed cream of mushroom soup, undiluted

1 can (10½ ounces) condensed cream of chicken soup, undiluted

1 can refrigerated buttermilk biscuits (8 biscuits), each biscuit cut into quarters

2 soup cans water

4 teaspoons all-purpose flour

2 teaspoons chicken bouillon granules

½ teaspoon black pepper

Combine chicken, soups, biscuits, water, flour, bouillon and pepper in **CROCK-POT®** slow cooker; stir to blend. Cover; cook on LOW 4 to 6 hours.

Tip: Don't add water to the **CROCK-POT®** slow cooker, unless the recipe specifically says to do so. Foods don't lose as much moisture during slow cooking as they can during conventional cooking, so follow the recipe guidelines for best results.

Creamy Chicken

Makes 3 servings

3 boneless, skinless chicken breasts *or* 6 boneless, skinless chicken thighs

2 cans (10½ ounces *each*) condensed cream of chicken soup, undiluted

1 can (about 14 ounces) chicken broth

1 can (4 ounces) sliced mushrooms, drained

½ medium onion, diced

   Salt and black pepper

   Hot cooked egg noodles (optional)

Combine chicken, soup, broth, mushrooms, onion, salt and pepper in **CROCK-POT®** slow cooker. Cover; cook on LOW 6 to 8 hours. Serve over noodles, if desired.

Hot and Sour Chicken

Makes 4 to 6 servings

4 to 6 boneless, skinless chicken breasts (1 to 1½ pounds total)

1 cup chicken or vegetable broth

1 package (about 1 ounce) dry hot-and-sour soup mix

Sugar snap peas and chopped red bell pepper (optional)

Sliced green onions (optional)

1. Place chicken in **CROCK-POT®** slow cooker; add broth and dry soup mix. Cover; cook on LOW 5 to 6 hours.

2. Serve over peas and bell peppers, if desired. Garnish with green onions.

Nice 'n' Easy Italian Chicken

Makes 4 servings

4 boneless, skinless chicken breasts (about 1 pound)

2 cans (4 ounces *each*) sliced mushrooms, drained

1 medium green bell pepper, chopped

1 medium zucchini, diced

1 medium onion, chopped

1 jar (26 ounces) pasta sauce

   Hot cooked linguini or spaghetti (optional)

Combine chicken, mushrooms, bell pepper, zucchini, onion and pasta sauce in **CROCK-POT®** slow cooker. Cover; cook on LOW 6 to 8 hours. Serve over linguini, if desired.

BOUNTIFUL BEEF

Fantastic Pot Roast

Makes 6 servings

2½ pounds boneless beef chuck roast

1 can (12 ounces) cola

1 bottle (10 ounces) chili sauce

2 cloves garlic

Hot cooked hominy and green beans (optional)

Combine beef, cola, chili sauce and garlic in **CROCK-POT**® slow cooker; turn beef to coat. Cover; cook on LOW 6 to 8 hours. Serve with sauce, hominy and beans, if desired.

Maple-Glazed Meatballs

Makes about 48 meatballs

1½ cups ketchup

1 cup maple syrup

⅓ cup soy sauce

1 tablespoon quick-cooking tapioca

1½ teaspoons ground allspice

1 teaspoon dry mustard

2 packages (about 16 ounces *each*) frozen fully cooked meatballs, partially thawed and separated

1 can (20 ounces) pineapple chunks in juice, drained

1. Combine ketchup, maple syrup, soy sauce, tapioca, allspice and dry mustard in **CROCK-POT®** slow cooker. Carefully stir meatballs and pineapple chunks into ketchup mixture. Cover; cook on LOW 5 to 6 hours.

2. Stir before serving. Serve warm with cocktail picks, if desired.

Tip: For a quick main dish, serve meatballs over hot cooked rice.

Easy Beef Burgundy

Makes 4 to 6 servings

1½ pounds boneless beef round steak, cut into 1-inch pieces

1 can (10¾ ounces) condensed cream of mushroom soup, undiluted

1 cup dry red wine

1 onion, chopped

1 can (4 ounces) sliced mushrooms, drained

1 package (about 1 ounce) dry onion soup mix

1 tablespoon minced garlic

Hot cooked egg noodles and asparagus (optional)

Combine beef, mushroom soup, wine, onion, mushrooms, dry soup mix and garlic in **CROCK-POT®** slow cooker; stir to blend. Cover; cook on LOW 6 to 8 hours. Serve over noodles with asparagus, if desired.

Easy Beef Burgundy

Hot and Juicy
Reuben Sandwiches

Makes 4 servings

1 corned beef, trimmed (about 1½ pounds)

2 cups sauerkraut, drained

½ cup beef broth

1 small onion, sliced

1 clove garlic, minced

¼ teaspoon caraway seeds

4 to 6 whole black peppercorns

8 slices pumpernickel or rye bread

4 slices Swiss cheese

Prepared mustard

Potato chips (optional)

1. Combine corned beef, sauerkraut, broth, onion, garlic, caraway seeds and peppercorns in **CROCK-POT®** slow cooker. Cover; cook on LOW 7 to 9 hours.

2. Remove beef to large cutting board. Cut beef across grain into slices. Divide among 4 bread slices. Top each slice with drained sauerkraut mixture and 1 slice cheese. Spread mustard on remaining 4 bread slices; place on sandwiches. Serve with chips, if desired.

Brisket with Sweet Onions

Makes 10 servings

2 large sweet onions, cut into 10 (½-inch) slices*

1 flat-cut boneless beef brisket (about 3½ pounds)

 Salt and black pepper

2 cans (about 14 ounces *each*) beef broth

1 teaspoon cracked black peppercorns

¾ cup crumbled blue cheese (optional)

Preferably Maui, Vidalia or Walla Walla onions.

1. Coat inside of **CROCK-POT®** slow cooker with nonstick cooking spray. Layer onions, beef, salt, black pepper, broth and peppercorns in **CROCK-POT®** slow cooker. Cover; cook on HIGH 5 to 7 hours.

2. Remove brisket to large cutting board. Cover loosely with foil; let stand 10 to 15 minutes. Slice evenly against the grain into ten slices. To serve, arrange onions on serving platter and spread slices of brisket on top. Sprinkle with blue cheese, if desired. Serve with cooking liquid.

Brisket with Sweet Onions

Best-Ever Roast

Makes 6 to 8 servings

4 to 5 medium potatoes, unpeeled and quartered

4 cups baby carrots

1 can (10¾ ounces) condensed cream of mushroom soup, undiluted

1 package (about 1 ounce) dry onion soup mix

1 boneless beef chuck shoulder roast (3 to 5 pounds)*

Unless you have a 5-, 6- or 7-quart **CROCK-POT® slow cooker, cut any roast larger than 2½ pounds in half so it cooks completely.*

Combine potatoes, carrots, mushroom soup and dry soup mix in **CROCK-POT**® slow cooker. Place roast in **CROCK-POT**® slow cooker. Cover; cook on LOW 4 to 6 hours.

Meatballs in Burgundy Sauce

Makes 6 to 8 servings

60 frozen fully cooked meatballs, partially thawed and separated

3 cups chopped onions

1½ cups water

1 cup Burgundy or other dry red wine

2 packages (about 1 ounce *each*) beef gravy mix

¼ cup ketchup

1 tablespoon dried oregano

Hot cooked egg noodles (optional)

Combine meatballs, onions, water, wine, gravy mix, ketchup and oregano in **CROCK-POT®** slow cooker; stir to blend. Cover; cook on LOW 8 to 10 hours or on HIGH 4 to 5 hours. Serve meatballs over noodles, if desired.

Serving Suggestion: Meatballs may also be served as an appetizer with remaining sauce as a dip.

Corned Beef and Cabbage

Makes 10 servings

12 small new potatoes, quartered

4 carrots, sliced

1 boneless beef brisket (about 2 pounds)

1 head cabbage, cut into wedges

2 medium yellow onions, sliced

3 whole bay leaves

8 whole black peppercorns

½ teaspoon pickling spice

1. Place potatoes and carrots in bottom of **CROCK-POT®** slow cooker. Add beef, cabbage, onions, bay leaves, peppercorns, pickling spice and enough water to cover brisket. Cover; cook on LOW 4 to 5 hours or on HIGH 2 to 2½ hours.

2. Remove brisket to large cutting board. Cover loosely with foil; let stand 10 to 15 minutes before slicing. Remove and discard bay leaves. Serve with vegetables.

Corned Beef and Cabbage

Shredded Beef Fajitas

Makes 6 servings

1 boneless beef flank steak (about 1½ pounds), cut into 6 pieces

1 can (about 14 ounces) diced tomatoes with mild green chiles

1 cup chopped onion

1 medium green bell pepper, chopped

2 cloves garlic, minced *or* ¼ teaspoon garlic powder

1 package (about 1½ ounces) fajita seasoning mix

12 (8-inch) flour tortillas

Optional toppings: chopped fresh cilantro, guacamole and/or shredded Cheddar cheese

1. Combine beef, tomatoes, onion, bell pepper, garlic and fajita seasoning mix in **CROCK-POT®** slow cooker. Cover; cook on LOW 8 to 10 hours or on HIGH 4 to 5 hours.

2. Remove beef to large cutting board; shred with two forks. Stir shredded beef back into **CROCK-POT®** slow cooker. Divide beef evenly among tortillas. Top as desired.

Peppered Beef Tips

Makes 2 to 3 servings

1 pound boneless beef round tip roast or round steak, cut into
1- to 1½-inch cubes

1 can (10¾ ounces) condensed French onion soup, undiluted

1 can (10¾ ounces) condensed cream of mushroom soup,
undiluted

2 cloves garlic, minced

Black pepper

Hot cooked rice (optional)

Combine beef, soups, garlic and pepper in **CROCK-POT®** slow
cooker; stir to blend. Cover; cook on LOW 8 to 10 hours. Serve over
rice, if desired.

Easy Beef Stroganoff

Makes 4 to 6 servings

3 cans (10¾ ounces *each*) condensed cream of mushroom soup, undiluted

2 pounds cubed beef stew meat

1 cup sour cream

½ cup water

1 package (1 ounce) dry onion soup mix

Hot cooked wild rice (optional)

Combine soup, beef, sour cream, water and dry soup mix in **CROCK-POT®** slow cooker; stir to blend. Cover; cook on LOW 6 hours or on HIGH 3 hours. Serve over rice, if desired.

Smothered Beef Patties

Makes 8 servings

Worcestershire sauce

Garlic powder

Salt and black pepper

1 can (about 14 ounces) Mexican-style diced tomatoes with
mild green chiles, undrained

8 frozen beef patties, unthawed

1 onion, cut into 8 slices

Hot cooked mashed potatoes (optional)

Layer bottom of **CROCK-POT®** slow cooker with small amount of
Worcestershire sauce, garlic powder, salt, pepper and 2 tablespoons
tomatoes. Add 1 beef patty. Top with small amount of Worcestershire,
garlic powder, salt, pepper, 2 tablespoons tomatoes and 1 onion slice.
Repeat layers seven times. Cover; cook on LOW 8 hours. Serve over
potatoes, if desired.

PLEASING PORK

Pork Tenderloin with Cabbage

Makes 6 servings

  3 cups shredded red cabbage

  ¼ cup chopped onion

  ¼ cup chicken broth

  1 clove garlic, minced

  1½ pounds pork tenderloin

  ¾ cup apple juice concentrate

  3 tablespoons honey mustard

  1½ tablespoons Worcestershire sauce

1. Add cabbage, onion, broth and garlic to **CROCK-POT®** slow cooker. Place pork over cabbage mixture. Pour apple juice concentrate, mustard and Worcestershire sauce over pork. Cover; cook on LOW 6 to 8 hours or on HIGH 3 to 4 hours.

2. Remove pork to large cutting board; cover loosely with foil. Let stand 10 to 15 minutes before slicing. Serve pork with cabbage and cooking liquid.

Polska Kielbasa
with Beer and Onions
Makes 6 to 8 servings

1 can (18 ounces) brown ale or beer

2 kielbasa sausages (16 ounces *each*), cut into 4-inch pieces

2 onions, quartered

⅓ cup packed dark brown sugar

⅓ cup honey mustard

Combine ale, sausages, onions, brown sugar and honey mustard in **CROCK-POT®** slow cooker; stir to blend. Cover; cook on LOW 4 to 5 hours.

Bacon and Cheese
Brunch Potatoes
Makes 6 servings

1 package (32 ounces) diced potatoes

1 cup chopped onion

½ teaspoon seasoned salt

4 slices bacon, crisp-cooked and crumbled

1 cup (4 ounces) shredded sharp Cheddar cheese

1 tablespoon water

1. Coat inside of **CROCK-POT®** slow cooker with nonstick cooking spray.

2. Place half of potatoes in **CROCK-POT®** slow cooker. Sprinkle half of onion and seasoned salt over potatoes; top with half of bacon and cheese. Repeat layers, ending with cheese. Sprinkle water over top.

Beans with Smoky Canadian Bacon

Makes 4 servings

2 cans (about 14 ounces *each*) diced fire-roasted tomatoes

1 can (about 15 ounces) pinto beans, rinsed and drained

1 package (8 ounces) Canadian bacon, cut into ½-inch cubes

½ cup Texas-style barbecue sauce*

1 small onion, finely chopped

½ teaspoon salt

⅛ teaspoon red pepper flakes

Black pepper

Cornbread (optional)

Look for barbecue sauce with liquid smoke as an ingredient.

Combine tomatoes, beans, Canadian bacon, barbecue sauce, onion, salt, red pepper flakes and black pepper in **CROCK-POT**® slow cooker. Cover; cook on LOW 5 to 7 hours. Serve with cornbread, if desired.

Glazed Pork Loin

Makes 4 servings

1 bag (1 pound) baby carrots

4 boneless pork loin chops

1 jar (8 ounces) apricot preserves

Place carrots on bottom of **CROCK-POT**® slow cooker. Place pork on top; spread with preserves. Cover; cook on LOW 8 hours or on HIGH 4 hours.

Beans with Smoky Canadian Bacon

Slow-Cooked Pork and Sauerkraut

Makes 6 servings

3 pounds boneless pork loin roast*

2 jars (32 ounces *each*) sauerkraut, rinsed and drained

2½ cups water

1 package (about 1 ounce) dry onion soup mix

3 tablespoons brown mustard

*Unless you have a 5-, 6- or 7-quart **CROCK-POT**® slow cooker, cut any roast larger than 2½ pounds in half so it cooks completely.*

Combine pork, sauerkraut, water, dry soup mix and mustard in **CROCK-POT**® slow cooker. Cover; cook on LOW 8 hours.

Sweet and Spicy Sausage Rounds

Makes about 16 servings

1 pound kielbasa sausage, cut into ¼-inch-thick rounds

⅔ cup blackberry jam

⅓ cup steak sauce

1 tablespoon yellow mustard

½ teaspoon ground allspice

Combine sausage, jam, steak sauce, mustard and allspice in **CROCK-POT®** slow cooker; stir to blend. Cover; cook on HIGH 3 hours.

Harvest Ham Supper

Makes 6 servings

6 carrots, cut into 2-inch pieces

3 medium sweet potatoes, quartered

1 to 1½ pounds boneless ham

1 cup maple syrup

Cornbread (optional)

Layer carrots, potatoes, ham and syrup in **CROCK-POT®** slow cooker. Cover; cook on LOW 6 to 8 hours. Serve with cornbread, if desired.

Big Al's Hot and Sweet Sausage Sandwiches

Makes 8 to 10 servings

4 to 5 pounds hot Italian sausage links

1 jar (26 ounces) pasta sauce

1 large Vidalia onion (or other sweet onion), sliced

1 green bell pepper, sliced

1 red bell pepper, sliced

¼ cup packed dark brown sugar

Italian rolls, cut in half

Provolone cheese, sliced (optional)

1. Combine sausages, pasta sauce, onion, bell peppers and brown sugar in **CROCK-POT®** slow cooker. Cover; cook on LOW 8 to 10 hours or on HIGH 4 to 6 hours.

2. Place sausages on rolls. Top with vegetable mixture. Add cheese, if desired.

Knockwurst and Cabbage

Makes 8 servings

8 to 10 knockwurst sausage links, cut into halves

1 head red cabbage, cut into ¼-inch slices

4 cups chicken broth

½ cup thinly sliced white onion

2 teaspoons caraway seeds

1 teaspoon salt

Chopped fresh Italian parsley (optional)

Combine, sausage, cabbage, broth, onion, caraway seeds and salt in **CROCK-POT®** slow cooker. Cover; cook on LOW 4 hours or on HIGH 2 hours. Garnish with parsley.

Simply Delicious Pork Roast

Makes 6 servings

1½ pounds boneless pork loin, cut into 6 pieces *or* 6 boneless pork loin chops

4 medium Golden Delicious apples, peeled and sliced

3 tablespoons packed brown sugar

1 teaspoon ground cinnamon

½ teaspoon salt

Combine pork, apples, brown sugar, cinnamon and salt in **CROCK-POT®** slow cooker. Cover; cook on LOW 6 to 8 hours.

Pork Roast
with Dijon Tarragon Glaze

Makes 4 to 6 servings

1½ to 2 pounds boneless pork loin, trimmed

⅓ cup chicken or vegetable broth

2 tablespoons *each* Dijon mustard and lemon juice

1 teaspoon *each* minced fresh tarragon and ground paprika

½ teaspoon black pepper

Sprigs fresh tarragon (optional)

Lemon slices (optional)

1. Combine pork, broth, mustard, lemon juice, minced tarragon, paprika and pepper in **CROCK-POT®** slow cooker. Cover; cook on LOW 6 to 8 hours or on HIGH 3 to 4 hours.

2. Remove roast to large cutting board. Cover loosely with foil; let stand 10 to 15 minutes before slicing. Serve with cooking liquid. Garnish with tarragon sprigs and lemon slices.

Country-Style Ribs

Makes 4 to 6 servings

    4 to 6 bone-in country-style pork ribs (2 to 3 pounds), trimmed

    2 cups water

1½ cups chopped onion

    1 bottle (20 to 24 ounces) ketchup

    1 jar (about 16 ounces) unsweetened applesauce

    2 tablespoons packed brown sugar

    ½ teaspoon hot pepper sauce (optional)

    Salt and black pepper

Combine pork, water, onion, ketchup, applesauce, brown sugar, hot pepper sauce, if desired, salt and black pepper in **CROCK-POT®** slow cooker; turn ribs to coat. Cover; cook on LOW 6 to 8 hours. Serve sauce over ribs.

Mango Ginger Pork Roast

Makes 4 to 6 servings

1 pork shoulder roast (about 4 pounds)*

2 cups mango salsa

2 tablespoons honey

¼ cup apricot preserves

½ to 1 teaspoon ground ginger

Salt and black pepper

Hot cooked rice (optional)

*Unless you have a 5-, 6- or 7-quart **CROCK-POT**® slow cooker, cut any roast larger than 2½ pounds in half so it cooks completely.*

Combine pork, salsa, honey, preserves, ginger, salt and pepper in **CROCK-POT**® slow cooker. Cover; cook on LOW 6 to 8 hours. Turn **CROCK-POT**® slow cooker to HIGH. Cover; cook on HIGH 3 to 4 hours. Serve with rice, if desired.

Pizza-Style Mostaccioli

Makes 4 servings

1 jar (24 to 26 ounces) marinara sauce or tomato basil pasta
    sauce

2 cups (6 ounces) uncooked mostaccioli pasta

1 package (8 ounces) sliced mushrooms

½ cup water

1 small yellow or green bell pepper, finely diced

½ cup (1 ounce) sliced pepperoni, halved

1 teaspoon dried oregano

¼ teaspoon red pepper flakes

1 cup (4 ounces) shredded pizza cheese blend or Italian
    cheese blend (optional)

Chopped fresh oregano (optional)

Garlic bread (optional)

1. Coat inside of **CROCK-POT®** slow cooker with nonstick cooking spray.

2. Combine marinara sauce, pasta, mushrooms, water, bell pepper, pepperoni, oregano and red pepper flakes in **CROCK-POT®** slow cooker; stir to blend. Cover; cook on LOW 2 hours or on HIGH 1 hour.

3. Stir well. Cover; cook on LOW 1½ to 2 hours or on HIGH 45 minutes to 1 hour. Garnish with cheese and fresh oregano. Serve with bread, if desired.

Old-Fashioned Sausage and Sauerkraut

Makes 8 to 10 servings

2 packages (19 ounces *each*) bratwurst

2 pounds sauerkraut

1 large head cabbage *or* 2 small heads cabbage

2½ cups chopped onion

8 slices bacon, crisp-cooked and chopped

4 tablespoons (½ stick) butter

2 tablespoons sugar

Salt and black pepper

Combine bratwurst, sauerkraut, cabbage, onion, bacon, butter, sugar, salt and pepper in **CROCK-POT®** slow cooker. Cover; cook on LOW 4 to 5 hours or on HIGH 1 to 3 hours.

Company Slow Cooker Pork Chops

Makes 4 to 6 servings

4 to 6 pork loin chops, cut ¾ inch thick

1 jar (2½ ounces) sliced dried beef

2 cans (10¾ ounces *each*) condensed cream of mushroom soup, undiluted

1 package (3 ounces) cream cheese, softened

½ cup milk

¼ cup sour cream

Black pepper

Steamed asparagus and potato wedges (optional)

1. Coat inside of **CROCK-POT®** slow cooker with nonstick cooking spray.

2. Layer half of pork and half of beef in **CROCK-POT®** slow cooker. Top with half of soup, cream cheese, milk, sour cream and pepper. Layer remaining half of pork and half of beef; top with remaining half of soup, cream cheese, milk, sour cream and pepper. Cover; cook on LOW 8 to 9 hours. Serve with asparagus and potatoes, if desired.

SPECTACULAR SIDES

Macaroni and Cheese

Makes 6 to 8 servings

6 cups cooked elbow macaroni

2 tablespoons butter

6 cups (24 ounces) shredded Cheddar cheese

4 cups evaporated milk

2 teaspoons salt

½ teaspoon black pepper

Toss macaroni with butter in large bowl. Stir in cheese, evaporated milk, salt and pepper. Remove to **CROCK-POT®** slow cooker. Cover; cook on HIGH 2 to 3 hours.

Variations: You may like to add diced green or red bell pepper, peas, hot dog slices, chopped tomato, browned ground beef or chopped onion for some tasty mix-ins.

Scalloped Tomatoes and Corn

Makes 4 to 6 servings

1 can (14¾ ounces) cream-style corn

1 can (about 14 ounces) diced tomatoes

¾ cup saltine or soda cracker crumbs

1 egg, lightly beaten

2 teaspoons sugar

¾ teaspoon black pepper

Chopped fresh tomatoes and Italian parsley (optional)

Combine corn, diced tomatoes, cracker crumbs, egg, sugar and pepper in **CROCK-POT**® slow cooker; stir to blend. Cover; cook on LOW 4 to 6 hours. Sprinkle with fresh tomatoes and parsley before serving, if desired.

Candied Sweet Potatoes

Makes 4 servings

3 medium sweet potatoes (1½ to 2 pounds), sliced into ½-inch rounds

½ cup water

¼ cup (½ stick) butter, cubed

2 tablespoons sugar

1 tablespoon vanilla

1 teaspoon ground nutmeg

Combine sweet potatoes, water, butter, sugar, vanilla and nutmeg in **CROCK-POT**® slow cooker; stir to blend. Cover; cook on LOW 7 hours or on HIGH 4 hours.

Green Onion-Bacon Creamed Corn

Makes 8 servings

2 packages (12 ounces *each*) frozen corn

4 slices bacon, crisp-cooked and crumbled, divided

1 cup chopped green onions

¾ cup whipping cream

4 teaspoons sugar

½ teaspoon salt

Coat inside of **CROCK-POT®** slow cooker with nonstick cooking spray. Stir in corn, half of bacon, green onions, whipping cream, sugar and salt. Cover; cook on LOW 4 to 4½ hours. Garnish each serving with remaining half of bacon.

Busy-Day Rice

Makes 4 servings

2 cups water

1 cup uncooked converted rice

2 tablespoons butter

1 tablespoon dried minced onion

1 tablespoon dried parsley flakes

2 teaspoons chicken bouillon granules

Combine water, rice, butter, onion, parsley and bouillon in **CROCK-POT®** slow cooker; stir to blend. Cover; cook on HIGH 2 hours.

Variations: During the last 30 minutes of cooking, add ½ cup green peas, broccoli florets or diced carrots.

Red Cabbage and Apples

Makes 6 servings

1 small head red cabbage, cored and thinly sliced

1 large apple, peeled and grated

¾ cup sugar

½ cup red wine vinegar

1 teaspoon ground cloves

Fresh apple slices (optional)

Combine cabbage, grated apple, sugar, vinegar and cloves in
CROCK-POT® slow cooker; stir to blend. Cover; cook on HIGH
6 hours. Garnish with apple slices.

Slow-Roasted Potatoes

Makes 3 to 4 servings

16 small new red potatoes, unpeeled

3 tablespoons butter, cubed

1 teaspoon paprika

½ teaspoon salt

¼ teaspoon garlic powder

Black pepper

Combine potatoes, butter, paprika, salt, garlic powder and pepper in **CROCK-POT®** slow cooker; stir to blend. Cover; cook on LOW 7 hours or on HIGH 4 hours.

Creamy Red Pepper Polenta

Makes 4 to 6 servings

6 cups boiling water

2 cups yellow cornmeal

1 small red bell pepper, finely chopped

¼ cup (½ stick) butter, melted

2 teaspoons salt

¼ teaspoon paprika, plus additional for garnish

⅛ teaspoon ground red pepper

⅛ teaspoon ground cumin

    Red bell pepper strips (optional)

Combine water, cornmeal, chopped bell pepper, butter, salt, ¼ teaspoon paprika, ground red pepper and cumin in **CROCK-POT®** slow cooker; stir to blend. Cover; cook on LOW 3 to 4 hours or on HIGH 1 to 2 hours. Garnish with additional paprika and bell pepper strips.

Cheesy Slow Cooker Potatoes

Makes 6 servings

1 bag (32 ounces) shredded hash brown potatoes

2 cans (10½ ounces *each*) condensed Cheddar cheese soup, undiluted

1 can (12 ounces) evaporated milk

1 cup chopped onion

Combine potatoes, soup, evaporated milk and onion in **CROCK-POT®** slow cooker; stir to blend. Cover; cook on LOW 6 to 8 hours.

Lemon and Tangerine Glazed Carrots

Makes 10 to 12 servings

6 cups sliced carrots

1½ cups apple juice

6 tablespoons butter

¼ cup packed brown sugar

2 tablespoons grated lemon peel

2 tablespoons grated tangerine peel

½ teaspoon salt

Chopped fresh Italian parsley (optional)

Combine carrots, apple juice, butter, brown sugar, lemon peel, tangerine peel and salt in **CROCK-POT®** slow cooker; stir to blend. Cover; cook on LOW 4 to 5 hours or on HIGH 1 to 3 hours. Garnish with parsley.

Savory Lentils

Makes 6 servings

3 cups chicken broth

1 cup dried brown lentils, rinsed and sorted

1 small yellow onion, chopped

1 stalk celery, trimmed and chopped

1 large carrot, chopped

¼ teaspoon dried thyme

Salt and black pepper

¼ cup chopped walnuts (optional)

1. Combine broth, lentils, onion, celery, carrot, thyme, salt and pepper in **CROCK-POT®** slow cooker; stir to blend. Cover; cook on HIGH 3 hours or until liquid is absorbed.

2. Spoon lentils into serving bowls. Sprinkle each serving evenly with walnuts, if desired.

Slow-Good Apples and Carrots

Makes 6 servings

6 carrots, sliced into ½-inch slices

4 apples, peeled, cored and sliced

½ cup orange juice

¼ cup plus 1 tablespoon all-purpose flour

1 tablespoon packed brown sugar

1 tablespoon butter, cubed

½ teaspoon ground nutmeg

Combine carrots, apples, orange juice, flour, brown sugar, butter and nutmeg in **CROCK-POT®** slow cooker. Cover; cook on LOW 3½ to 4 hours.

Brussels Sprouts
with Bacon, Thyme and Raisins

Makes 8 servings

2 packages (12 ounces *each*) frozen Brussels sprouts

1 cup chicken broth

⅔ cup golden raisins

2 thick slices applewood smoked bacon, chopped

2 tablespoons chopped fresh thyme

Trim ends from sprouts; cut in half lengthwise through core (or in quarters), if desired. Combine sprouts, broth, raisins, bacon and thyme in **CROCK-POT®** slow cooker; stir to blend. Cover; cook on LOW 3 to 4 hours.

Collard Greens

Makes 10 servings

2 packages (16 ounces *each*) chopped collard greens

2 cups water

½ medium red bell pepper, cut into strips

⅓ medium green bell pepper, cut into strips

¼ cup olive oil

Salt and black pepper

Combine collard greens, water, bell peppers, oil, salt and black pepper in **CROCK-POT®** slow cooker; stir to blend. Cover; cook on LOW 3 to 4 hours or on HIGH 2 hours or until heated through.

BBQ Baked Beans

Makes 12 servings

3 cans (about 15 ounces *each*) white beans, drained

4 slices bacon, chopped

¾ cup prepared barbecue sauce

½ cup maple syrup

1½ teaspoons ground mustard

1. Coat inside of **CROCK-POT®** slow cooker with nonstick cooking spray.

2. Add beans, bacon, barbecue sauce, maple syrup and ground mustard; stir to blend. Cover; cook on LOW 4 hours.

SWEET TREATS

Pumpkin-Cranberry Custard

Makes 4 to 6 servings

1 can (30 ounces) pumpkin pie filling

1 can (12 ounces) evaporated milk

1 cup dried cranberries

4 eggs, beaten

1 cup whole gingersnap cookies (optional)

Combine pumpkin, evaporated milk, cranberries and eggs in **CROCK-POT**® slow cooker; stir to blend. Cover; cook on HIGH 4 to 4½ hours. Serve with gingersnaps, if desired.

Apple and Granola Breakfast Cobbler

Makes 4 servings

4 medium Granny Smith apples, peeled, cored and sliced

2 cups granola cereal, plus additional for garnish

½ cup packed light brown sugar

2 tablespoons butter, cubed

1 tablespoon lemon juice

1 teaspoon ground cinnamon

Whipping cream, half-and-half or yogurt (optional)

Combine apples, 2 cups granola, brown sugar, butter, lemon juice and cinnamon in **CROCK-POT**® slow cooker. Cover; cook on LOW 6 hours or on HIGH 2 to 3 hours. Serve warm. Garnish with additional granola and cream.

Easy Chocolate Pudding Cake

Makes about 16 servings

1 package (6-serving size) instant chocolate pudding
and pie filling mix

3 cups milk

1 package (about 18 ounces) chocolate fudge cake mix plus
ingredients to prepare mix

Whipped topping or ice cream (optional)

Crushed peppermint candies (optional)

1. Spray 4-quart **CROCK-POT®** slow cooker with nonstick cooking spray. Add pudding mix; whisk in milk.

2. Prepare cake mix according to package directions. Carefully pour cake mix into **CROCK-POT®** slow cooker. *Do not stir.* Cover; cook on HIGH 1½ hours or until cake is set. Serve warm with whipped topping, if desired. Garnish with candies.

Spiced Apple and Cranberry Compote

Makes 6 servings

2½ cups cranberry juice cocktail

1 package (6 ounces) dried apples

½ cup (2 ounces) dried cranberries

½ cup Rhine wine or apple juice

½ cup honey

2 whole cinnamon sticks, broken into halves

Frozen yogurt or ice cream (optional)

1. Combine juice, apples, cranberries, wine, honey and cinnamon stick halves in **CROCK-POT®** slow cooker; stir to blend. Cover; cook on LOW 4 to 5 hours or until liquid is absorbed and fruit is tender.

2. Remove and discard cinnamon sticks. Serve with yogurt, if desired.

Spiced Apple and Cranberry Compote

Homestyle Apple Brown Betty

Makes 8 servings

6 cups of your favorite cooking apples, peeled,
cored and cut into eighths

1 cup dry bread crumbs

¾ cup packed brown sugar

½ cup (1 stick) butter, melted

¼ cup finely chopped walnuts

1 teaspoon *each* ground cinnamon and ground nutmeg

⅛ teaspoon salt

1. Coat inside of **CROCK-POT®** slow cooker with nonstick cooking spray.

2. Add apples, bread crumbs, brown sugar, butter, walnuts, cinnamon, nutmeg and salt; stir to blend. Cover; cook on LOW 3 to 4 hours or on HIGH 2 hours.

Tip: The ingredients can all be doubled and prepared in a 5-, 6- or 7-quart **CROCK-POT®** slow cooker.

Figs Poached in Red Wine

Makes 4 servings

2 cups dry red wine

1 cup packed brown sugar

12 dried Calimyrna or Mediterranean figs (about 6 ounces)

2 (3-inch) whole cinnamon sticks

1 teaspoon finely grated orange peel

4 tablespoons whipping cream (optional)

1. Combine wine, brown sugar, figs, cinnamon sticks and orange peel in **CROCK-POT®** slow cooker; stir to blend. Cover; cook on LOW 5 to 6 hours or on HIGH 4 to 5 hours.

2. Remove and discard cinnamon sticks. To serve, spoon figs and syrup into serving dish. Top with cream, if desired. Serve warm or cold.

Spicy Fruit Dessert

Makes 4 to 6 servings

2 cups canned pears, drained and diced

2 cups carambola (star fruit), sliced and seeds removed

1 can (6 ounces) frozen orange juice concentrate

¼ cup orange marmalade

¼ teaspoon pumpkin pie spice

Pound cake or ice cream (optional)

Whipped cream (optional)

Combine pears, carambola, orange juice concentrate, marmalade and pumpkin pie spice in **CROCK-POT**® slow cooker; stir to blend. Cover; cook on LOW 4 to 6 hours or on HIGH 2 to 3 hours. Serve warm over pound cake with whipped cream, if desired.

Whoa Breakfast

Makes 6 servings

3 cups water

2 cups chopped peeled apples

1½ cups steel-cut or old-fashioned oats

¼ cup sliced almonds

½ teaspoon ground cinnamon

Combine water, apples, oats, almonds and cinnamon in **CROCK-POT®** slow cooker. Cover; cook on LOW 8 hours.

"Peachy Keen" Dessert

Makes 8 to 12 servings

2 pounds fresh peaches (about 8 medium), sliced

1⅓ cups old-fashioned oats

1 cup granulated sugar

1 cup packed light brown sugar

⅔ cup buttermilk baking mix

2 teaspoons ground cinnamon

½ teaspoon ground nutmeg

Combine peaches, oats, sugars, baking mix, cinnamon and nutmeg in **CROCK-POT®** slow cooker; stir to blend. Cover; cook on LOW 4 to 6 hours.

Red Hot Applesauce

Makes 8 servings

10 to 12 apples, peeled, cored and chopped

¾ cup hot cinnamon candies

½ cup apple juice or water

Combine apples, candies and apple juice in **CROCK-POT®** slow cooker. Cover; cook on LOW 7 to 8 hours or on HIGH 4 hours.

Triple Chocolate Fantasy

Makes 36 pieces

2 pounds white almond bark, broken into pieces

1 bar (4 ounces) sweetened chocolate, broken into pieces*

1 package (12 ounces) semisweet chocolate chips

3 cups coarsely chopped pecans, toasted (optional)**

Use your favorite high-quality chocolate candy bar.

**To toast pecans, spread in single layer in heavy skillet. Cook and stir over medium heat 1 to 2 minutes or until nuts are lightly browned.*

1. Place bark, sweetened chocolate and chocolate chips in **CROCK-POT®** slow cooker. Cover; cook on HIGH 1 hour. *Do not stir.*

2. Turn **CROCK-POT®** slow cooker to LOW. Cover; cook on LOW 1 hour, stirring every 15 minutes.

3. Stir in nuts. Drop mixture by tablespoonfuls onto baking sheet covered with waxed paper; cool. Store in tightly covered container.

Variations: Here are a few ideas for other imaginative items to add in along with or instead of the pecans: raisins, crushed peppermint candy, candy-coated baking bits, crushed toffee, peanuts or pistachio nuts, chopped gum drops, chopped dried fruit, candied cherries, chopped marshmallows or sweetened coconut.

Five-Spice Apple Crisp

Makes 4 servings

- 3 tablespoons unsalted butter, melted

- 6 Golden Delicious apples, peeled and cut into ½-inch-thick slices

- 2 teaspoons lemon juice

- ¼ cup packed brown sugar

- ¾ teaspoon Chinese five-spice powder *or* ½ teaspoon ground cinnamon and ¼ teaspoon ground allspice, plus additional for garnish

- 1 cup coarsely crushed Chinese-style almond cookies or almond biscotti

  Sweetened whipped cream (optional)

1. Butter inside of 5-quart **CROCK-POT®** slow cooker with melted butter. Add apples and lemon juice; toss to combine. Sprinkle apples with brown sugar and ¾ teaspoon five-spice powder; toss again. Cover; cook on LOW 3½ hours.

2. Spoon into bowls. Sprinkle cookies over apples. Garnish with whipped cream and additional five-spice powder.

Pineapple Daiquiri Sundae Topping

Makes 4 to 6 servings

1 can (20 ounces) pineapple chunks, drained

½ cup sugar

½ cup dark rum

3 tablespoons lime juice

Peel of 2 limes, cut into long strips

1 tablespoon cornstarch

Ice cream, pound cake or shortcake (optional)

Fresh raspberries (optional)

1. Combine pineapple, sugar, rum, lime juice, lime peel and cornstarch in 1½-quart **CROCK-POT®** slow cooker; stir to blend. Cover; heat 3 hours or until warmed through.

2. Serve over ice cream, if desired. Garnish with raspberries.

A

Almonds: Whoa Breakfast, 133

Apple and Granola Breakfast Cobbler, 126

Autumn Chicken, 54

B

Bacon and Cheese Brunch Potatoes, 92

Barbecue

BBQ Baked Beans, 123

Beans with Smoky Canadian Bacon, 94

Best Barbecued Ribs, 14

Chicken Stew, 53

Root Beer BBQ Pulled Pork, 12

BBQ Baked Beans, 123

Beans

BBQ Baked Beans, 123

Beans with Smoky Canadian Bacon, 94

Black and White Chili, 38

Corn and Two Bean Chili, 52

Family Tortilla Bowl, 23

Mile-High Enchilada Pie, 65

Navy Bean and Ham Soup, 47

Rustic Vegetable Soup, 44

Beans with Smoky Canadian Bacon, 94

Beef, 72–89

Company Slow Cooker Pork Chops, 107

Easy Beef Stew, 46

Family Tortilla Bowl, 23

Mushroom-Beef Stew, 42

One Pot Meatloaf Dinner, 30

Swiss Steak Stew, 50

Tender Pot Roast, 8

Tomato Sauce with Meatballs and Sausage, 10

Veggie Soup with Beef, 40

Beer: Polska Kielbasa with Beer and Onions, 92

Best Barbecued Ribs, 14

Best-Ever Roast, 82

Big Al's Hot and Sweet Sausage Sandwiches, 99

Black and White Chili, 38

Brisket with Sweet Onions, 80

Brussels Sprouts with Bacon, Thyme and Raisins, 121

Busy-Day Rice, 113

C

Cabbage and Sauerkraut

Corned Beef and Cabbage, 84

Hot and Juicy Reuben Sandwiches, 78

Knockwurst and Cabbage, 100

Old-Fashioned Sausage and Sauerkraut, 106

Pork Tenderloin with Cabbage, 90

Red Cabbage and Apples, 114

Slow-Cooked Pork and Sauerkraut, 96

Candied Sweet Potatoes, 110

Carrots

Best-Ever Roast, 82

Chicken and Wild Rice Soup, 48

Corned Beef and Cabbage, 84

Easy Beef Stew, 46

Glazed Pork Loin, 94

Harvest Ham Supper, 98

Juicy Roasted Chicken, 34

Lemon and Tangerine Glazed Carrots, 118

Savory Lentils, 119

Simmered Split Pea Soup, 36

Slow-Good Apples and Carrots, 120

Cheesy Dump Pizza, 24

Cheesy Slow Cooker Chicken, 66

Cheesy Slow Cooker Potatoes, 116

Cherry Delight, 28

Chicken, 54–71

Black and White Chili, 38

Chicken and Wild Rice Soup, 48

Chicken Soft Tacos, 18

Chicken Stew, 53

Ginger Teriyaki Chicken, 22

Juicy Roasted Chicken, 34

Ranch Chicken and Stuffing, 26

Chicken and Butternut Squash, 61

Chicken and Rice, 60

Chicken and Wild Rice Soup, 48

Chicken in Enchilada Sauce, 56

Chicken in Honey Sauce, 62

Chicken Provençal, 66

Chicken Soft Tacos, 18

Chicken Stew, 53

Cinnamon Roll-Topped Mixed Berry
Cobbler, 16

Clam Chowder, 51

Collard Greens, 122

Company Slow Cooker Pork Chops, 107

Corn

Chicken in Enchilada Sauce, 56

Chicken Stew, 53

Clam Chowder, 51

Corn and Two Bean Chili, 52

Green Onion-Bacon Creamed Corn, 112

Navy Bean and Ham Soup, 47

Posole, 40

Scalloped Tomatoes and Corn, 110

Corn and Two Bean Chili, 52

Corned Beef and Cabbage, 84

Country-Style Ribs, 103

Creamy Chicken, 69

Creamy Red Pepper Polenta, 116

D

Dijon Chicken Thighs with Artichoke
Sauce, 64

E

Easy Beef Burgundy, 76

Easy Beef Stew, 46

Easy Beef Stroganoff, 88

Easy Chocolate Pudding Cake, 127

F

Family Tortilla Bowl, 23

Fantastic Pot Roast, 72

Figs Poached in Red Wine, 131

Fish and Shellfish: Clam Chowder, 51

Five-Spice Apple Crisp, 138

G

Ginger Teriyaki Chicken, 22

Glazed Pork Loin, 94

Green Onion-Bacon Creamed Corn, 112

H

Harvest Ham Supper, 98

Hearty Vegetable and Potato Chowder,
43

Homestyle Apple Brown Betty, 130

Hot and Juicy Reuben Sandwiches, 78

Hot and Sour Chicken, 70

J

Juicy Roasted Chicken, 34

K

Knockwurst and Cabbage, 100

L

Lemon and Tangerine Glazed Carrots,
118

Like Grandma's Chicken 'n' Dumplings,
68

M

Macaroni and Cheese, 108

Mango Ginger Pork Roast, 104

Maple-Glazed Meatballs, 74

Meatballs in Burgundy Sauce, 83

Mile-High Enchilada Pie, 65

Mushroom

Autumn Chicken, 54

Best-Ever Roast, 82

Company Slow Cooker Pork Chops, 107

Creamy Chicken, 69

Dijon Chicken Thighs with Artichoke Sauce, 64

Easy Beef Burgundy, 76

Easy Beef Stroganoff, 88

Hearty Vegetable and Potato Chowder, 43

Like Grandma's Chicken 'n' Dumplings, 68

Mushroom-Beef Stew, 42

Nice 'n' Easy Italian Chicken, 71

Peppered Beef Tips, 87

Pizza-Style Mostaccioli, 105

Smothered Pork Chops and Rice, 20

Mushroom-Beef Stew, 42

N

Navy Bean and Ham Soup, 47

Nice 'n' Easy Italian Chicken, 71

O

Oats

One Pot Meatloaf Dinner, 30

"Peachy Keen" Dessert, 134

Whoa Breakfast, 133

Old-Fashioned Sausage and Sauerkraut, 106

One Pot Meatloaf Dinner, 30

P

Pasta

Macaroni and Cheese, 108

Pizza-Style Mostaccioli, 105

"Peachy Keen" Dessert, 134

Peas: Simmered Split Pea Soup, 36

Peppered Beef Tips, 87

Pineapple

Maple-Glazed Meatballs, 74

Pineapple Daiquiri Sundae Topping, 139

Pineapple Daiquiri Sundae Topping, 139

Pizza-Style Mostaccioli, 105

Polska Kielbasa with Beer and Onions, 92

Pork, 90–107

BBQ Baked Beans, 123

Best Barbecued Ribs, 14

Brussels Sprouts with Bacon, Thyme and Raisins, 121

Clam Chowder, 51

Green Onion-Bacon Creamed Corn, 112

Navy Bean and Ham Soup, 47

One Pot Meatloaf Dinner, 30

Posole, 40

Root Beer BBQ Pulled Pork, 12

Simmered Split Pea Soup, 36

Smothered Pork Chops and Rice, 20

Tomato Sauce with Meatballs and Sausage, 10

Pork Roast with Dijon Tarragon Glaze, 102

Pork Tenderloin with Cabbage, 90

Posole, 40

Potato (see also **Potatoes, Sweet**)

Bacon and Cheese Brunch Potatoes, 92

Best-Ever Roast, 82

Cheesy Slow Cooker Potatoes, 116

Chicken Stew, 53

Potato (continued)

Clam Chowder, 51

Corned Beef and Cabbage, 84

Easy Beef Stew, 46

Hearty Vegetable and Potato Chowder, 43

Juicy Roasted Chicken, 34

One Pot Meatloaf Dinner, 30

Rustic Vegetable Soup, 44

Slow-Roasted Potatoes, 115

Potatoes, Sweet

Candied Sweet Potatoes, 110

Harvest Ham Supper, 98

Pumpkin-Cranberry Custard, 124

R

Ranch Chicken and Stuffing, 26

Red Cabbage and Apples, 114

Red Hot Applesauce, 135

Rice

Busy-Day Rice, 113

Chicken and Rice, 60

Chicken and Wild Rice Soup, 48

Ginger Teriyaki Chicken, 22

Smothered Pork Chops and Rice, 20

Root Beer BBQ Pulled Pork, 12

Rustic Vegetable Soup, 44

S

Salsa

Corn and Two Bean Chili, 52

Mango Ginger Pork Roast, 104

Mile-High Enchilada Pie, 65

Spicy Shredded Chicken, 62

Savory Lentils, 119

Scalloped Tomatoes and Corn, 110

Shredded Beef Fajitas, 86

Simmered Split Pea Soup, 36

Simply Delicious Pork Roast, 100

Slow-Cooked Pork and Sauerkraut, 96

Slow-Good Apples and Carrots, 120

Slow-Roasted Potatoes, 115

Smothered Beef Patties, 89

Smothered Pork Chops and Rice, 20

Spiced Apple and Cranberry Compote, 128

Spicy Fruit Dessert, 132

Spicy Orange Chicken Nuggets, 58

Spicy Shredded Chicken, 62

Squash

Chicken and Butternut Squash, 61

Nice 'n' Easy Italian Chicken, 71

Pumpkin-Cranberry Custard, 124

Sweet and Spicy Sausage Rounds, 97

Swiss Steak Stew, 50

T

Tender Pot Roast, 8

Tomato Sauce with Meatballs and Sausage, 10

Triple Chocolate Brownies, 32

Triple Chocolate Fantasy, 136

V

Veggie Soup with Beef, 40

W

Walnuts

Cherry Delight, 28

Homestyle Apple Brown Betty, 130

Whoa Breakfast, 133

Wine

Autumn Chicken, 54

Easy Beef Burgundy, 76

Figs Poached in Red Wine, 131

Meatballs in Burgundy Sauce, 83

Spiced Apple and Cranberry Compote, 128

Metric Conversion Chart

VOLUME MEASUREMENTS (dry)

¹/₈ teaspoon = 0.5 mL
¹/₄ teaspoon = 1 mL
¹/₂ teaspoon = 2 mL
³/₄ teaspoon = 4 mL
1 teaspoon = 5 mL
1 tablespoon = 15 mL
2 tablespoons = 30 mL
¹/₄ cup = 60 mL
¹/₃ cup = 75 mL
¹/₂ cup = 125 mL
²/₃ cup = 150 mL
³/₄ cup = 175 mL
1 cup = 250 mL
2 cups = 1 pint = 500 mL
3 cups = 750 mL
4 cups = 1 quart = 1 L

VOLUME MEASUREMENTS (fluid)

1 fluid ounce (2 tablespoons) = 30 mL
4 fluid ounces (¹/₂ cup) = 125 mL
8 fluid ounces (1 cup) = 250 mL
12 fluid ounces (1¹/₂ cups) = 375 mL
16 fluid ounces (2 cups) = 500 mL

WEIGHTS (mass)

¹/₂ ounce = 15 g
1 ounce = 30 g
3 ounces = 90 g
4 ounces = 120 g
8 ounces = 225 g
10 ounces = 285 g
12 ounces = 360 g
16 ounces = 1 pound = 450 g

DIMENSIONS

¹/₁₆ inch = 2 mm
¹/₈ inch = 3 mm
¹/₄ inch = 6 mm
¹/₂ inch = 1.5 cm
³/₄ inch = 2 cm
1 inch = 2.5 cm

OVEN TEMPERATURES

250°F = 120°C
275°F = 140°C
300°F = 150°C
325°F = 160°C
350°F = 180°C
375°F = 190°C
400°F = 200°C
425°F = 220°C
450°F = 230°C

BAKING PAN SIZES

Utensil	Size in Inches/Quarts	Metric Volume	Size in Centimeters
Baking or	8×8×2	2 L	20×20×5
Cake Pan	9×9×2	2.5 L	23×23×5
(square or	12×8×2	3 L	30×20×5
rectangular)	13×9×2	3.5 L	33×23×5
Loaf Pan	8×4×3	1.5 L	20×10×7
	9×5×3	2 L	23×13×7
Round Layer	8×1½	1.2 L	20×4
Cake Pan	9×1½	1.5 L	23×4
Pie Plate	8×1¼	750 mL	20×3
	9×1¼	1 L	23×3
Baking Dish	1 quart	1 L	—
or Casserole	1½ quart	1.5 L	—
	2 quart	2 L	—